IMPROVISATION
on the ii-V7-I
& BLUES
PROGRESSIONS
For the Beginner and Beyond

By: David J. Rice

Edited by: Dr. Kathleen Briseno

To the biggest BRAT in the whole entire world, who has dedicated his life to music and his students.

Dave, you will leave behind a gift to the world of wonderful, talented musicians of all ages.   In turn, they will carry on your legacy of creating and appreciating music of all styles. Your contribution has helped to keep music alive in the voices, hands and hearts of the young and old.

Thank you for your gift.

PREFACE

This book is a method of study for the beginning music student who desires to learn to improvise his/her instrument in a jazz or blues idiom. This book includes two CDs.

The ii-V-I progression and blues progression are the most important progressions for the beginning music student. There are variations of the ii-V-I progression which we will also explore in this study. Each chord progression, scale, chord voicing, arpeggio, and melody may be practiced with a slow, medium, and fast audio track to allow the student to gain proficiency.

This tutorial includes several written music examples that have been written for concert instruments, Bb instruments, Eb instruments, and F instruments. The music examples have been written in such a way that the student may play his/her instrument reading the appropriate transposed score and it will match the audio example which accompanies.

CONTENTS

INTRODUCTION

The study method I have created includes a written text with illustrations and audio CDs. The student learns improvisation beginning with simple melodies played over ii-V-I chord progressions. Each step in learning to play melodies and harmonies is accompanied with slow, medium, and fast audio recordings to allow the beginning student to start slowly and gain confidence and proficiency. As the student becomes familiar with one level they advance to more complex melodies, scales, and chords. This method may be used by the beginning elementary student and the more complex scales and harmonies may be used by the junior high and high school student.

At this juncture, I should mention that I have studied piano since the age of 6 and played in bands since the age of 10. My first paid job was in Junior High School. My friends and I took our rock n'roll band and played for a nighttime dance for students in the "Happy Day" Home for children with mental deficiencies. We earned $5 each. Since that day I have always played in at least one or two bands at a time. Upon beginning my college undergraduate education I found I could make a decent part time living while in school by playing jobs with other music majors. After graduation, I immediately went on the road with several diverse groups ranging from jazz, pop, disco, blues, rock n'roll, funk, country, and show music. I had already been practicing ii-V-I chord progressions for several years when Jamie Abersold came to give a clinic to our jazz band at SIU, Carbondale. I have an immense respect for the instruction and knowledge that he and others have given to our modern day music field.

While many authors have written fine books for the high school and college level student, their beginning point is too high for my younger students who are just learning music for the first time in their life. My goal was to create a method of study that any age student can understand. Opening with the fundamentals; the simplest melody which will fit over a ii-V-I chord progression and advancing to more challenging scales and arpeggios.

METHOD

There are lots of chord progressions, but ii-V-I is the most common chord progression jazz musicians play. The original source of the ii,V, and I chords are the modes of the major scale. Think of the modes this way: The C major scale has seven different notes, and you can play the scale starting on any one of its seven notes. This means that there are really seven different C major scales- one that starts on C, one on D, one on E, one on F, and so on through B. Each mode has a Greek name, shown to the right of the mode. The Roman numerals I through VII shown to the left of each mode correspond to the modal name on the right- I is Ionian, II is Dorian, III is Phrygian, and so forth. This is the same in every major key.

Greek modal names are not esoteric; they are everyday terms that jazz musicians use. From the modes come seventh chords. Seventh chords are constructed by playing every other note of each mode.

This book will explore the ii-V7-I chord progressions, and other related chord progressions. We will also study the blues progression. We will begin at an elementary level of practicing scales and chords and advance to more difficult levels step by step.

If you are a beginning musician you already have a little bit of ability to play on your instrument. We will begin by showing examples of chord progressions, and then explore how to play improvisatory notes over the progressions. At first you may think, This doesn't sound like something I've heard. Please allow time to develop the progressions, learn the scales, alternate voicings and alternate progressions. Eventually, you will be able to develop an entire vocabulary of improvisatory techniques to use in playing your instrument.

Extremely Important: Rule #1

At this point, I would like you to get into the habit of practicing everything that you learn in all 12 keys on your instrument. Each time you gain a little snippet of information or learn a new solo riff it will feel like a blinder has fallen off your eyes and ears. You will most likely play this newfound riff in a song that you are practicing and be very happy to have it in that song. To truly imbed this line, chord structure, or riff in your grey matter you must now turn and practice in all of its applications in all keys.

Lesson 1: ii-V-I

We will start with the ii-V7- I progression. We are starting in the key of C major though it is important to keep in mind these principles can apply to the same chord progression in other keys as well. In the key of C major, a C major chord is the I chord. Roman numerals will be used to indicate the position of the chord on the major or minor scale. In C major we call the C –I; we call D minor –ii; we call E minor iii; we call F major IV; we call G major V; we call A minor vi; and we call B diminished vii°. In the I major chord there is a Major 3rd (4 half steps) between the root (name of the chord) and the 3rd. There is a minor 3rd (3 half steps between the 3rd and the 5th).

The following chart indicates the relationship in our beginning chords between the roots, 3rds and 5ths. M3 indicates Major 3rd; m3 indicates minor 3rd.

Chord	Root	Interval	3rd	Interval	5th
I	C	M3	E	m3	G
ii	D	m3	F	m3	A
iii	E	m3	G	M3	B
IV	F	M3	A	m3	C
V	G	M3	B	m3	D
vi	A	m3	C	M3	E
viiø	B	m3	D	m3	F

In the ii-V- I progression we play D minor, G major, then C major. If you play guitar or keyboards play music example #1. Next, you should take example #1 and play it in all 12 keys. Before we begin, you should note that the 2nd chord in each example is in first inversion. This means that the 3rd of the chord is on the bottom which sounds smoother and makes the transition between the other chords smoother.

Dan Haerle gives some really great tips for chord voicings for the pianist, guitarist, or vibraphonist. In connecting chords, individual chord tones should move smoothly to a tone in the next chord, usually stepwise. Common tones between two successive chords may be retained or moved stepwise if a resolution causes duplication of a tone (Haerle,1974,p.iii).

Exercise: #1a: ii-V-I Practice in every key

Here is Music Example 1 in all twelve keys. You will notice that this corresponds to the Audio Ex.1 ii-V-I slow, Audio Ex.1 ii-V-I Medium and Audio Ex. 1 ii-V-I fast on the CD. If you play a polyphonic rhythm instrument like piano, organ, guitar, or vibraphones, play along with music Ex.1.

Exercise: #1b: ii-V-I Practice arpeggios in every key

If you play a linear instrument that is in concert key, for example flute or violin, please refer to the following music exercise which is arpeggios of the ii-V-I progression for concert instruments. Audio music example #1 (ii-V-I slow) is where you should start. Play the simple melody over Audio Music Example #1 (ii-V-I in all keys). As you become more confident move to Music Example #2 (ii-V-I Medium). Eventually you can play Audio Music Example #3 (ii-V-I Fast).

The above version of Exercise 1b is for Bb instruments. If you play Bb trumpet, or any of the Bb brass instruments or Bb woodwinds like tenor saxophone you should read the following Bb version of the Exercise 1. It has been transposed so that as you read the exercise you can play along with Audio Example #1 slow, medium, or fast.

If you play an Eb instrument like alto saxophone the following exercise is transposed
So that as you play the written exercise it will align with the Audio Example #1 Slow, Example #2 Medium, or
Example # 3 Fast.

Our last arpeggio exercise is written for F instruments. Please refer to the following exercise for F instruments. As
you read this it will align with Audio Exercise #1 slow, medium, or fast.

There is a relationship of a perfect fourth between D minor and G and there is also a perfect fourth between G the dominant and C the I –called the tonic. When you play the chord progression ii-V-I there is a "tension" from ii-V and the tension is released when you finally play the I chord. Always listen for the "tension" as you play this progression because the tension will affect how you improvise and what you play. Later, we will speak more about the tension and release of musical lines, the tension created by musical intervals, and tension within chord progressions. Please refer to music example #1,2, and 3.

There is a strong urgency to resolve the V chord to the I. This is created by the B natural which is a leading tone. Our B leading tone is urging us to move it upward one half step to the tonic-C. We can use this "urgency" or "tension" to create interest when we are soloing.

Lesson 2: Modes

Modes are scales which are lines of notes in 2nds and/or 3rds ascending or descending. Modes are "inversions" of the Major scale. This means that all of the following modes are Diatonic to the C major scale.

D Dorian mode is the inversion of C Major (also called Ionian). D Dorian plays the notes of the C major scale except that instead of starting on C, it starts on D –thus acquiring its name D Dorian E, Phrygian mode plays from E to E encompassing the notes of the C major scale.   F, Lydian encompasses the notes of the C major scale from F to F. The G MixoLydian mode encompasses the diatonic tones of the C Major scale from G to G. The A, Aeolian mode encompasses the diatonic tones of the C Major scale from A to A, and the B, Locrian mode encompasses the diatonic tones of the C major scale from B to B (Mode, n.d.).

The next objective will be to familiarize ourselves with the D minor scale which is called the Dorian mode. Soloists use the Dorian mode frequently in improvisation. The reason I start with the Dorian mode is to familiarize yourself with the scale which you probably will use over a ii chord more often than other scales. Let's observe and play along with the Dorian mode on concert instruments with the Audio track as follows:

DAVE RICE

DORIAN MODE 12 KEYS CONCERT INST.

Next, we will play the Dorian mode with the audio exercise on Bb instruments.

DAVE RICE

DORIAN MODE 12 KEYS Bb INST.

Next, we will play the Dorian mode with the audio exercise on Eb instruments.

DAVE RICE

DORIAN MODE 12 KEYS Eb INST.

Lastly, we will play the Dorian mode with the audio exercise on F instruments.

We will now proceed to practice the remaining modes in this order: Ionian, Phrygian. Lydian, MixoLydian, Aeolian, Locrian. The following music pages when read will align with the CD which is enclosed with the packet. Please notice that following the concert keys there is a page for you to practice if you play a Bb instrument, then a page if you play an Eb instrument and finally an F instrument.

IONIAN MODE CONCERT

PHRYGIAN MODE CONCERT

LYDIAN MODE CONCERT

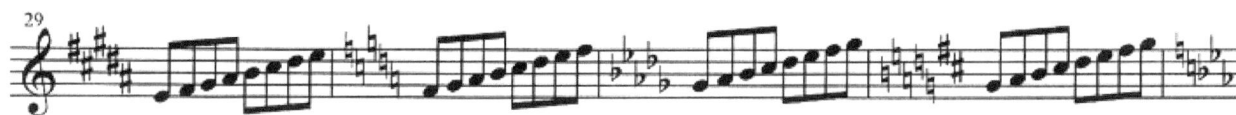

MIXOLYDIAN MODE CONCERT

AEOLIAN MODE CONCERT

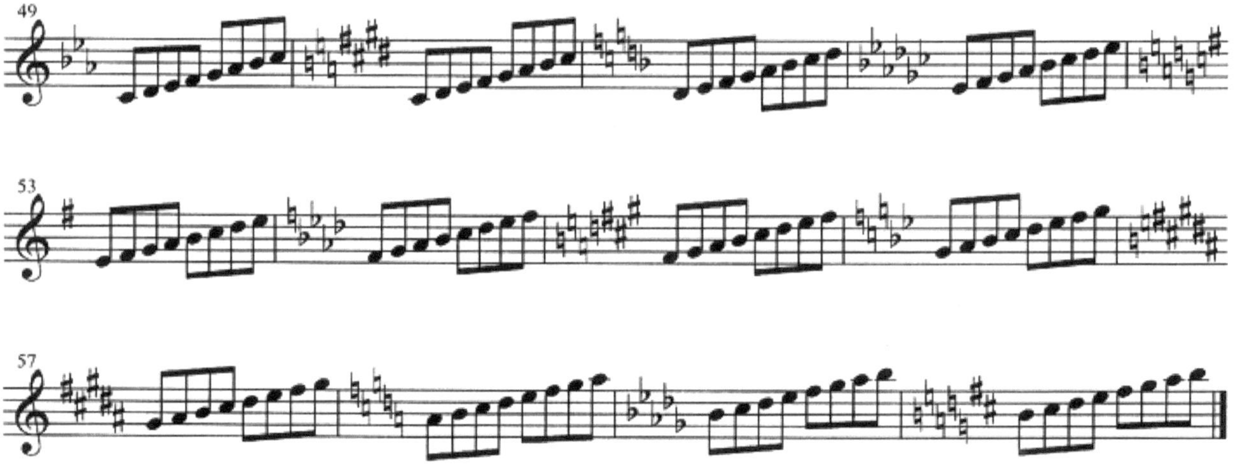

LOCRIAN MODE CONCERT

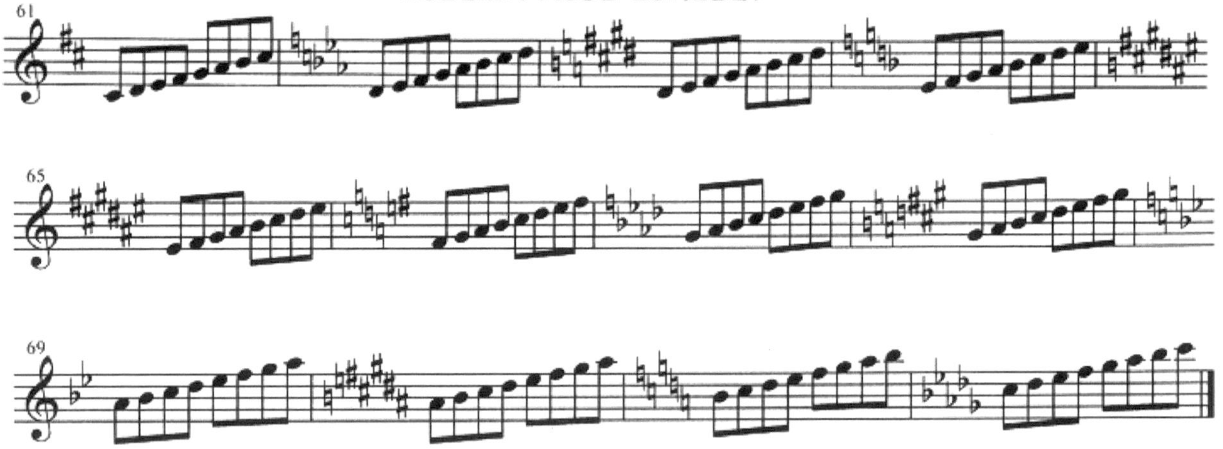

IONIAN MODE Bb INSTRUMENTS

PHRYGIAN MODE Bb INSTRUMENTS

LYDIAN MODE Bb INSTRUMENTS

MIXOLYDIAN MODE Bb INSTRUMENTS

AEOLIAN MODE B♭ INSTRUMENTS

LOCRIAN MODE B♭ INSTRUMENTS

IONIAN MODE Eb INSTRUMENTS

PHRYGIAN MODE Eb INSTRUMENTS

LYDIAN MODE Eb INSTRUMENTS

MIXOLYDIAN MODE Eb INSTRUMENTS

AEOLIAN MODE Eb INSTRUMENTS

LOCRIAN MODE Eb INSTRUMENTS

Ionian Mode F Instruments

Phrygian Mode F Instruments

LYDIAN MODE F INSTRUMENTS

MIXOLYDIAN MODE F INSTRUMENTS

AEOLIAN MODE F INSTRUMENTS

LOCRIAN MODE F INSTRUMENTS

The musical modes that are diatonic to the C major scale are related as follows.

C	Ionian (C Major)	C	D	E	F	G	A	B	C					
D	Dorian		D	E	F	G	A	B	C	D				
E	Phrygian			E	F	G	A	B	C	D	E	F		
F	Lydian				F	G	A	B	C	D	E	F		
G	MixoLydian					G	A	B	D	E	F	G		
A	Aeolian						A	B	C	D	E	F	G	A
B	Locrian							B	C	D	E	F	G	A	B

Extremely Important: Rule #2

Try playing each mode as a separate scale and try not to rely on your current knowledge of the major scale as a crutch. With the modes in front of you, think of them as separate scales unto themselves. The beginning student will rely on the major scale as a point of orientation. You must think of the Dorian mode on D as its own scale- a type of D minor scale. You must think of the E Phrygian mode as its own E minor scale. To do this, practice the Dorian mode in all 12 keys on your instrument. As you are playing the scale, say the name out loud-ie-G Dorian, Bb MixoLydian, F# Locrian. This practice will help you to call on the modes as a source of tonal improvisation when the harmonic chord structure supports the use of that particular mode.

Exercise: #2: Practice modes in every key

First practice the Dorian mode in every key. The reason I have started with the Dorian mode and not Ionian is to pique the interest of the young musician who may feel a little overwhelmed or frustrated at this point. The first scales that I experimented with as a youth in 5th and 6th grade were the minor based Dorian and Aeolian modes. Next practice the Ionian mode in each of twelve keys. Then practice the Phrygian mode in each of twelve keys. Go through all the modes until you have completed all 7 modes. You now have 84 scales at your disposal for use in improvising. As I stated earlier, the modes as listed above line up with the audio tracks on CDs enclosed.

Lesson 3: Chord Voicings

In this lesson we will understand how chords are constructed and how they are named. A chord is simply two or more notes played together at the same time. When a piano player strikes two or more notes on a piano or when a guitar player plays two or more notes on the guitar we have a chord.

The chord is named by intervals of 3rds. An interval is the distance between two notes. Recall that in lesson 1 we had a table of chords used in the diatonic major scale. We showed that there is an interval (or distance) between the root and the 3rd, and between the 3rd and the 5th tones of the scale. For demonstration purposes, in the key of C Major between C the root, and E we have an interval of a Major 3rd (4 ½ steps). Between E the third and G the fifth we have an interval of a minor 3rd. This creates a chord called a C major triad, the C root giving the chord its name.

There are four types of triads, which we will encounter. They are major, minor, diminished and augmented.

Major Chord	Root (name of Chord) to 3rd	Major 3rd	4 half Steps
	3rd to 5th	minor 3rd	3 half Steps
Minor Chord	Root (name of Chord) to 3rd	minor 3rd	3 half Steps
	3rd to 5th	Major 3rd	4 half Steps
Diminished Chord	Root (name of Chord) to 3rd	minor 3rd	4 half Steps
	3rd to 5th	minor 3rd	4 half Steps
Augmented Chord	Root (name of Chord) to 3rd	Major 3rd	4 half Steps
	3rd to 5th	Major 3rd	4 half Steps

Thus far we have looked at triads. We shall now go beyond the triad to the next interval above the fifth which is called the seventh. The seventh is seven scale tones above the root of the chord. There are 2 types of sevenths found in chords- the major seventh and the minor seventh. A major seventh is 11 half steps above the root, while the minor seventh is 10 half steps above the root.

When we refer to a seventh chord, the triad will already be understood by the name of the chord.

▪ A seventh chord (also called a dominant seventh chord) consists of a Major triad with a minor 7th on top. The minor seventh is 10 half steps above the root.
▪ A minor 7th chord consists of a minor triad with a minor 7th on top. The minor seventh is 10 half steps above the root.
▪ A Major 7th chord consists of a Major triad with a major 7th on top. The major seventh is 11 half steps above the root.
▪ A half diminished chord also called m7(b5) has a diminished triad with a minor seventh. The minor seventh is 10 half steps above the root.
▪ A seventh chord with Aug.5 has an augmented triad with a minor 7th.
▪ A minor chord major7 has exactly what it says. A minor triad with major 7th.

Dan Haerle writes in his book "Jazz/Rock voicings for the contemporary Keyboard Player:" The 3rd and/or the 7th of the chord should normally be present in every voicing.

In progressions of a 5th downward (4th upward), the following is always true:
▪ The 3rd of a chord has the same letter name as the 7th of the next but may require a chromatic alteration.
▪ The 7th of a chord should normally resolve downward stepwise to the 3rd of the next chord (Haerle,1974,p.iii).

Exercise: #3a: Practice ii7-V7-I chord progressions in every key

Play ii7-V7-I chord progressions in all 12 keys using a minor seventh chord for the ii, using a dominant seventh chord for the V7, and using a Major seventh chord for the I chord. This will familiarize you with using voicings between chord changes. Through experimentation you will find that you can leave out certain voices in the chord. Often a left hand can play just the root, 3rd, and 7th of the minor seventh chord, producing an open cleaner sound. Experiment and determine what sounds you like the best.

Play along with Exercise #1 first slowly, and then build up speed using the chord voicings in this following chart. This chart appears only in concert because it pertains to polyphonic chordal concert instruments.
Lesson #4 Playing Scales over chord voicings

We are now at a major crossroad. Now is when we are really ready to begin improvising over chord voicings. This is really the crux of what playing jazz, blues, rock 'n roll, country, Dixieland, funk, some pop, gospel, swing, and other styles are all about.

We will start at a very easy level and work our way through to more advanced methods. From this point forward you should establish a daily ritual of practicing ii-V7-I chord progressions in all 12 keys incorporating the voicings and lines that you will learn from this point forward. I really saw a profound difference in my own playing when I began to practice these progressions on a daily basis in all 12 keys.

Exercise: #3b: Elementary Improvisation Over ii-V-I

We will begin with an elementary improvisation of the first 3 tones of the Dorian Mode over the ii chord, followed by the first 3 tones of the MixoLydian Mode over the V chord, followed by the first 3 tones of the Ionian Mode over the I chord. Practice this easy improvisation in use of scales over the Exercise # 1, which is ii-V-I Slow. D Dorian scale- D,E, and F played over the D minor 7th chord followed by G,A, and B over the G7 chord, followed by C,D, and E over the C major chord is the first progression. If you play piano, you should voice the chords in the left hand and play improvised melody in the right hand. Do not play bass notes in the left hand. If you play another instrument, play the notes we just cited over the recording provided with this series. The notes D, E and F are the simplest melody using the D Dorian mode G, A, and B the simplest using the MixoLydian Mode and C, D, and E are the simplest using the Ionian. Now play Ex.3b in Concert and the keys Bb, Eb, and F.

iim7-V7-IMAJ7 WITH SIMPLE MELODY   DAVE RICE

iim7-V7-IMaj7 with simple melody Bb Inst.

DAVE RICE

iim7-V7-IMaj7 with simple melody Eb Inst.

DAVE RICE

iim7-V7-IMaj7 with simple melody F Inst.

DAVE RICE

Exercise: #3c: Practice full mode over ii7-V7-I

Now let's play the full mode over the same slow chord progression, using the slowest recording of ii-V-I . Use Exercise #3 slow. This will take you through all 12 keys so you must transpose the same melody line in other keys. The F7 is now the V7 chord Play F G A Bb C D EbF over the F7 V chord. When you resolve the V7 to the I (Bb), play the Bb Ionian or Major scale over the Bb. This downward transposition continues in whole steps until you end on D major. Then begin the ii-V7-I progression in the key of Db. In so doing you play Eb F Gb Ab Bb C Db Eb over the Eb ii7, Ab Bb C Db Eb F Gb Ab as the Ab MixoLydian over the Ab7 chord and Db Ionian over the Db major which is the I chord. Each time you move downward one whole step you are shifting the I chord down one step and thus your entire progression. This forces you as a player to play and apply these scales in all twelve keys. It will hone your harmonic skills and your ear training skills at the same time.

In the scope of jazz improvisation this is a very 'consonant' sounding improvisation and you may think it sounds a little plain. Go ahead and practice these modes because our next step will take us into much more interesting tonality. At this time, play the following notes with Exercise #3 on the CD on the slowest speed. The following concert music score is for guitar, vibes, piano, organ, etc. Following it will be Bb instruments, Eb instruments, and F instruments.

FULL MODES OVER II7-V7-I CONCERT — DAVE RICE

FULL MODES OVER II7-V7-I B♭

DAVE RICE

FULL MODES OVER II7-V7-I E♭

DAVE RICE

FULL MODES OVER II7-V7-I F

DAVE RICE

Lesson 4: The Minor Chords and the Altered Scale

Hopefully, you have been practicing the minor ii- V7-I progression. This is a relatively simple progression with the modes used to play over the chords. Next, we will explore more complex chord changes and more possibilities of scales and voicings to use. In songs that are written in minor keys the triad over the first scale tone- the i chord is minor. (eg. In the key of C minor -C Eb G). Additionally, the ii chord has a third and a fifth that is flat. This results in a ii¯7 chord called a half diminished 7 chord. This means that the triad is diminished and the seventh is a minor 7th above the root of the chord. D F Ab C spells the half diminished chord. If we follow our progression we will also find that the V chord is actually a V+7 which is the abbreviation for G B D# F a V augmented with a minor seventh. The triad itself is augmented and the seventh is a minor seventh. This chord has a strong sense of needing to resolve to a minor triad over the i chord, which is spelled C Eb G. Looking at the voicings of ii¯7 to V+7 to I minor in all keys, we notice that the first six progressions of two measures each only include half the keys. Therefore, we must practice the entire progression one half step higher starting in the key of Db minor(C# minor). This progression winds around ending in the key of Eb minor. The Eb minor is the same as D# minor, so as you end the second chord progression exercise you switch from flats back into sharps.

Lesson 5: Diminished, Half Diminished, Altered and Blues Scales

As we are about to look at this progression there are three very important scales which fit wonderfully over the ii¯7 to V+7 to I minor. These are the Diminished Scales, Half Diminished Scales and Altered Scales. Also important are the Minor Pentatonic and Blues Scales. The diminished scale is simply alternating whole and half steps. The diminished and half diminished scales are really inversions of one another. As you practice the scales you will discover that at every minor third the scale begins to repeat itself. You will also see that the half diminished scale is the same as a diminished scale simply starting on the second tone of the diminished scale. Many people consider the Half Diminished scale to be the same as the Locrian mode. The notes of the Locrian mode cover the tones of the minor 7 flat 5 chord. Those tones include the root, minor 3rd, flatted 5th and minor 7th. The Half Diminished Scale which is spelled C C# D# E F# G A Bb C also covers the same tones which are included in a Cm7b5. The sound is slightly different because this scale includes both the minor and major third in the chord. It also includes a major 6th above the root as opposed to a minor 6th which occurs in the Locrian mode. Your own preference will dictate which scale you use in improvisation. For the scope of this paper we will use the scale spelled with alternating half and whole steps as the Half Diminished. There are plenty of instructional materials available using the Locrian mode. Here are the Diminished, Half Diminished, Minor Pentatonic, Blues, and Altered Scales.

DIMINISHED SCALES

ILLUSTRATED BY DAVE RICE

HALF DIMINISHED SCALES

MINOR PENTATONIC

ALTERED SCALE

BLUES SCALE

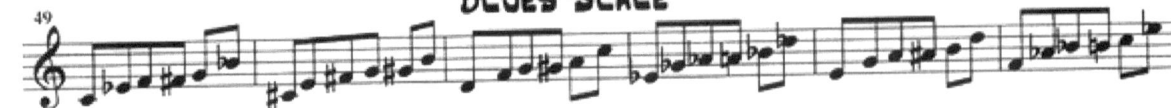

For example if we start on C and examine each diminished scale in chromatic half steps we see:

C	D	Eb	F	F#	G#	A	B	C	
C#	D#	E	F#	G	A	Bb	C	C#	
D	E	F	G	Ab	Bb	B	C#	D	
Eb	F	F#	G#	A	B	C	D	Eb	Notice the same tones as the first scale
E	F#	G	A	Bb	C	C#	D#	E	Notice the same tones as the 2nd scale
F	G	Ab	Bb	B	C#	D	E	F	Notice the same tones as the 3rd scale
F#	G#	A	B	C	D	Eb	F	F#	Notice the same tones as the 4th scale
G	A	Bb	C	C#	D#	E	F#	G	Notice the same tones as the 5th scale
Ab	Bb	B	C#	D	E	F	G	AB	Notice the same tones as the 6th scale
A	B	C	D	Eb	F	F#	G#	A	Notice the same tones as the 7th scale
Bb	C	C#	D#	E	F#	G	A	Bb	Notice the same tones as the 8th scale
B	C#	D	E	F	G	Ab	Bb	B	Notice the same tones as the 9th scale

The next important scales to look at are the half diminished scales which are also alternating between half steps and whole steps. These scales will also be symmetrical and repeat the notes every minor third as you practice them chromatically.

C	C#	D#	E	F#	G	A	Bb	C	
C#	D	E	F	G	Ab	Bb	B	C#	
D	Eb	F	F#	G#	A	B	C	D	
Eb	E	F#	G	A	Bb	C	Db	Eb	Notice the same tones as the first scale
F	G	Ab	Bb	B	C#	D	E		Notice the same tones as the 2nd scale
F	F#	G#	A	B	C	D	Eb	F	Notice the same tones as the 3rd scale
F#	G	A	Bb	C	Db	Eb	E	F#	Notice the same tones as the 4th scale
G	Ab	Bb	B	C#	D	E	F	G	Notice the same tones as the 5th scale
G#	A	B	C	D	Eb	F	F#	G#	Notice the same tones as the 6th scale
A	Bb	C	Db	Eb	E	F#	G	A	Notice the same tones as the 7th scale
Bb	B	C#	D	E	F	G	Ab	Bb	Notice the same tones as the 8th scale
B	C	D	Eb	F	F#	G#	A	B	Notice the same tones as the 9th scale

Again, it must be emphasized that these scales are just alternating whole steps and half steps apart and that every minor 3rd they repeat each other. They are completely symmetrical. Also notice that the half diminished scale is just the same as the diminished scale starting one tone higher and therefore starting with a half step (or m2nd).

From this point forward for the rest of this presentation of ii-V7-I and ii-7 V+7 i, I would like you to practice these scales over the chord progressions of ii-V7-I and ii-7 V+7 i. If you play piano, organ, guitar, vibes, marimba or other polyphonic instruments practice chord voicings with scale lines over the chord voicings. If you play a linear instrument such as saxophone, trumpet, oboe, clarinet, etc. play the scales over the recorded ii-V7-I and ii-7 V+7-i exercises that come with this manual. This gives you an opportunity to hear the interaction between the scales and the chord changes. We will suggest certain scales over chords but it is very important that you now begin to experiment with and choose different scales and modes to play over the ii-V7-I and ii-7 V+7-i progressions.

Here is one combination of scales to try. We will play the diminished scale over the ii-7 chord and the half diminished over the V+7 chords, then a Minor Pentatonic over the I chord. The Minor Pentatonic is just 5 notes starting on the tonic C Eb F G Bb. Over C minor. It is really simply constructed out of the Dorian mode using the root, 3rd, 4th,5th and 7th tones of the Dorian mode. At this time play the Diminished scale starting on the ii-7, Half Diminished scale starting on the V7+, and the Minor Pentatonic scale starting on the i minor chord.

DIMINISHED HALF DIMINISHED OVER I♭7-V7+- I MINOR CONCERT

DAVE RICE

DIMINISHED HALF DIMINISHED OVER IIø7-V7+- I MINOR B♭
DAVE RICE
Eø7 A7+5 Dm7 Dø7 G7+5 Cm7
Cø7 F7+5 B♭m7 A♯ø7 D♯7+5 G♯m7
G♯ø7 C♯7+5 F♯m7 F♯ø7 B7+5 Em7
Fø7 B♭7+5 E♭m7 D♯ø7 G♯7+5 C♯m7
C♯ø7 F♯7+5 Bm7 Bø7 E7+5 Am7
Aø7 D7+5 Gm7 Gø7 C7+5 Fm7
DIMINISHED HALF DIMINISHED OVER IIø7-V7+- I MINOR E♭
Bø7 E7+5 Am7 Aø7 D7+5 Gm7
Gø7 C7+5 Fm7 Fø7 B♭7+5 E♭m7
D♯ø7 G♯7+5 C♯m7 C♯ø7 F♯7+5 Bm7
Cø7 F7+5 B♭m7 B♭ø7 E♭7+5 A♭m7

G#ø7 C#7+5 F#m7 F#ø7 B7+5 Em7
Eø7 A7+5 Dm7 Dø7 G7+5 Cm7
DIMINISHED HALF DIMINISHED OVER IIø7-V7+- I MINOR F
Aø7 D7+5 Gm7 Gø7 C7+5 Fm7
Fø7 Bb7+5 Ebm7 D#ø7 G#7+5 C#m7
C#ø7 F#7+5 Bm7 Bø7 E7+5 Am7
A#ø7 D#7+5 G#m7 G#ø7 C#7+5 F#m7
F#ø7 B7+5 Em7 Eø7 A7+5 Dm7
Dø7 G7+5 Cm7 Cø7 F7+5 Bbm7

Exercise: #5a: Experiment with Altered Scales

Now we will experiment with a scale called the **altered scale**. This is a scale which can be used over different chords but it is particularly useful over the V7 chord, or a chord which is being used as a dominant. The **altered scale** starts out like the half diminished scale ñ Ω step , whole step, Ω step up to the third and then it continues as a whole tone scale ñ ie- all whole steps up until you have reached the root again. So an altered scale played over a G7 chord would be spelled G,Ab,Bb,Cb(B),Db,Eb,F,G. Let's play an exercise over the ii-7 chord, V+7, and i minor. We will use the half diminished scale over the ii-7, an altered scale over the V7+ and a blues scale over the I minor.

Try this combination over the slowest ii-7-V7+-I minor audio exercise or you can play the same scales over the ii7-V7-I exercise.

HALF DIMINISHED, ALTERED, AND BLUES SCALE OVER IIø7 –V7+–I CONCERT

Dave Rice

HALF DIMINISHED, ALTERED, AND BLUES SCALE OVER iiø7 –V7+-I B♭

DAVE RICE

HALF DIMINISHED, ALTERED, AND BLUES SCALE OVER iiø7 –V7+-I E♭

HALF DIMINISHED, ALTERED, AND BLUES SCALE OVER iiø7 -V7+-I F
G#ø7 C#7+ F#m7 F#ø7 B7+ Em7
Eø7 A7+ Dm7 Dø7 G7+ Cm7
Aø7 D7+ Gm7 Gø7 C7+ Fm7
Fø7 B♭7+ E♭m7 D#ø7 G#7+ C#m7
C#ø7 F#7+ Bm7 Bø7 E7+ Am7
B♭ø7 E♭7+ A♭m7 G#ø7 C#7+ F#m7
F#ø7 B7+ Em7 Eø7 A7+ Dm7
Dø7 G7+ Cm7 Cø7 F7+ B♭m7

Lesson 6: Bitonality

Bitonality refers to two different tonal centers- thus the prefix ìbiî. We mostly use the bitonal harmonies on V7 chords although you will find it on other chords. As you play jazz and read charts you will see complex chords that have names like. C9 #11, D+5+9, F# b5b9, A+9#11. All of these chord symbols refer to raising and lowering the upper harmonies of the chord structure. Once you have established the 3rd, 5th, and 7th of the chord, the upper harmonies are listed separately in the symbol. As a matter of protocol, if the 3rd is not indicated it is understood to be a major 3rd above the root.

If an interval which is indicated in the chord is higher than the 7th, for example +9, b9,#11, b11, and the chord is a dominant 7th chord, then the 7th is understood to be a minor 7th above the root. To make this much more interesting, and perhaps easier, think of chords in jazz as having two parts: the upper and lower tone center. The lower tone center is the root, sometimes a third, sometimes a fifth and usually including the 7th. The upper harmony will include usually a 9th, sometimes an 11th, sometimes a 13th, and often the 5th which may have been omitted in the lower harmony. All of this will be indicated on music in a moment. When we view the chords as a lower and upper harmony we see that we can have a lower triadic harmony with the seventh and a completely different triad on top. This is very important because we can play the upper triad which is 'stacked' on top of the lower harmony, and we can solo on top of the upper harmony. This practice was widely used in the soloing of Charlie Parker and especially in the playing of artists such as Herbie Hancock and Michael Brecker. Before we list the upper triads to look for make sure that you practice the Diminished, Half Diminished, and Altered scales over the ii7-V7-I progressions and ii-7-V7+-i progressions in all twelve keys because these three scales will encompass all of the bitonal stacked harmonies we are about to talk about.

Exercise: #6a: Building Bitonal Chords

We will use the C chord as an example. You should realize that all chords can have the same stacked bitonal harmonies. Play C the root and Bb the 7th as the lower harmony in your left hand. Above this chord one may stack any of the chords in the whole tone scale above the root C. So, we may play a C triad over a C7. A D triad played over a C7 results in a #11, 13 chord. An E triad played over a C7 chord results in a Major 7 +5. A F# triad played over a C7 creates a C7 b5b9. A G# triad over a C7 results in a C7+5+9. A Bb triad over a C7 is called an 11 chord. Please note that often times when an 11th chord is played, the third is omitted because the 11th will clash with it. Also, other triads not found in the whole tone scale may be superimposed above a C7 chord. An A triad played over a C7 results in a C b9 13 chord. An Eb triad played over a C7 results in a +9 chord. Sometimes a composer will write the chord as G#/C or Eb/C. The writer finds that it is easier to simply list the two separate tonal centers. This now gives us a fresh approach to improvisation. Now when improvising over a chord, use all of the various scales practiced over the upper and lower harmonies which are suggested in the chord. When we combine all of the scales we have studied thus far and play them over either the upper or lower harmonies of the chordal structure we have hundreds of ideas to choose from in improvising over a jazz progression.

Below is a list of the chordal possibilities over just the C chord. It is up to you as a good studious musician to practice these in all the twelve keys. You have the ii7-V7-I and ii⁻7-V7+-i progressions to practice with. Start on the slowest speed and build your tempo up as you increase your skill in all twelve keys.

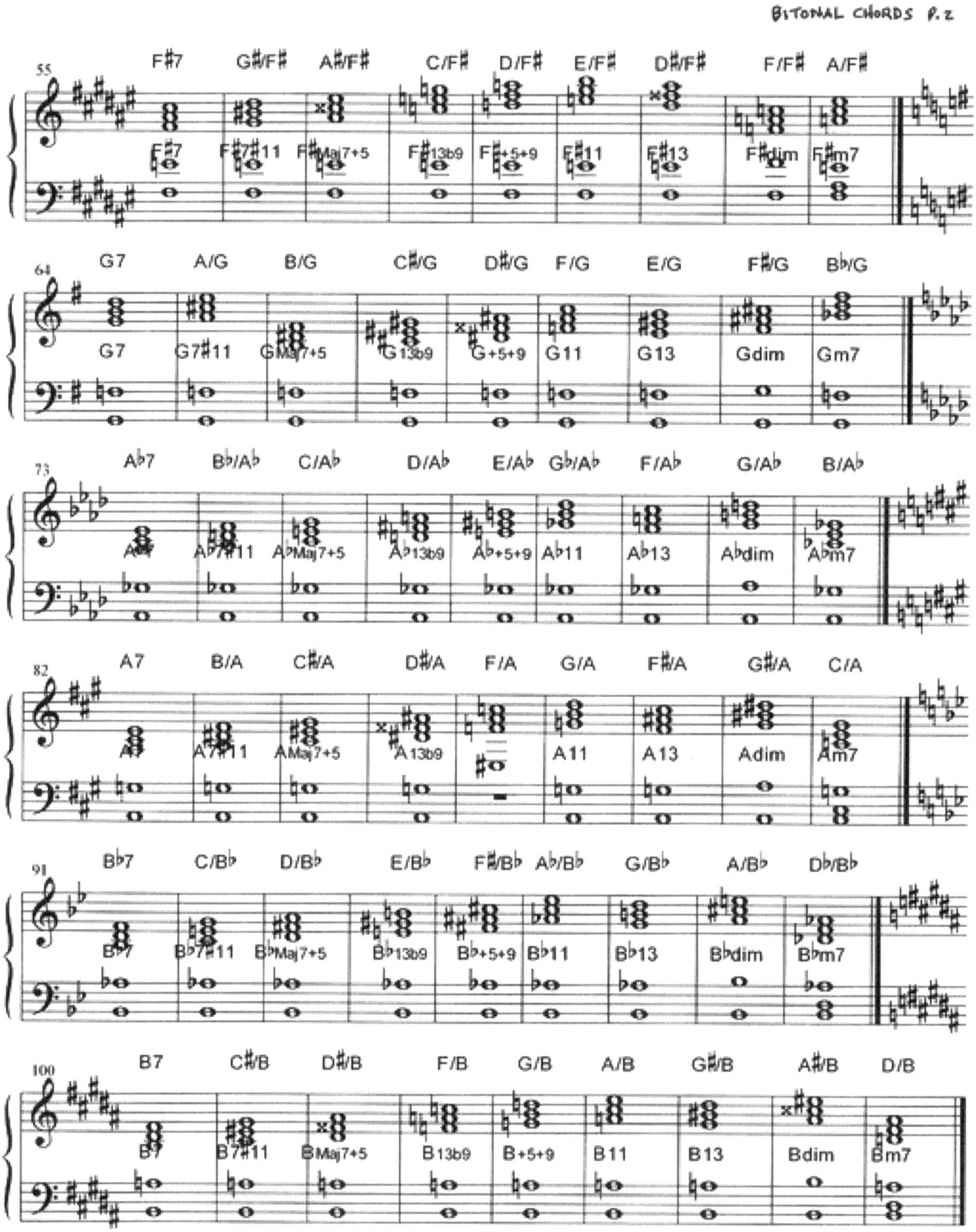
BITONAL CHORDS P.2
55
F♯7 G♯/F♯ A♯/F♯ C/F♯ D/F♯ E/F♯ D♯/F♯ F/F♯ A/F♯
F♯7 F♯7♯11 F♯Maj7+5 F♯13b9 F♯+5+9 F♯11 F♯13 F♯dim F♯m7
64
G7 A/G B/G C♯/G D♯/G F/G E/G F♯/G B♭/G
G7 G7♯11 GMaj7+5 G13b9 G+5+9 G11 G13 Gdim Gm7
73
A♭7 B♭/A♭ C/A♭ D/A♭ E/A♭ G♭/A♭ F/A♭ G/A♭ B/A♭
A♭7 A♭7♯11 A♭Maj7+5 A♭13b9 A♭+5+9 A♭11 A♭13 A♭dim A♭m7
82
A7 B/A C♯/A D♯/A F/A G/A F♯/A G♯/A C/A
A7 A7♯11 AMaj7+5 A13b9 A11 A13 Adim Am7
91
B♭7 C/B♭ D/B♭ E/B♭ F♯/B♭ A♭/B♭ G/B♭ A/B♭ D♭/B♭
B♭7 B♭7♯11 B♭Maj7+5 B♭13b9 B♭+5+9 B♭11 B♭13 B♭dim B♭m7
100
B7 C♯/B D♯/B F/B G/B A/B G♯/B A♯/B D/B
B7 B7♯11 BMaj7+5 B13b9 B+5+9 B11 B13 Bdim Bm7

Lesson 7: The Blues Progression

The next area that we will cover briefly, is the chord progression called the Blues Progression. This progression is tied into jazz so closely that the two cannot really be separated, and any study of jazz would be remiss in not having a section on the blues.

There are many deviations of the blues progression and anyone who listens to deep southern country blues will hear uneven numbers of measures and odd progressions, but in general there are two progressions which are most common. They are the I IV V7 progression which is a more common shuffle or rock progression, and the I IV V7 with a iii-VI ii V7 ñ I turnaround which we hear frequently in bebop. Earlier we listed the blues scale in the same illustration in which we saw the altered scale and diminished scale. The unique thing about the blues scale is that the minor third is used over a major chord creating the dissonant clash of minor against major, and that the fourth is used with the sharp or raised fourth into the fifth. With instruments like the saxophone or guitar the fourth and raised fourth can be bent upward into the fifth.

When you play blues you can play a straight progression like this one, which is a typical Country or West Side Chicago Blues progression: This progression is used frequently in Rockin' Roll Blues songs.

Exercise: #7a: Play a 12 bar blues progression in every key

```
|| C7  | F7  | C7  |C7  | F7  | F7  | C7  | C7  | G7  | F7  | C7 C/E F7 F#dim.| C7  G7 ||
||C#7  | F#7 | C#7 |C#7 | F#7 | F#7 | C#7 | C#7 | G#7 | F#7 | C#7 C#/E# F#7 Gdim.|C#7 G#7 |
||D7  |G7  | D7  |D7  |G7  | G7  | D7  |D7  | A7  | G7  | D7 D/F# G7 G#dim.| D7  A7 ||
||Eb7  | Ab7 | Eb7 |Eb7 | Ab7 | Ab7 |Eb7  | Eb7 | Bb7 | Ab7 | Eb Eb/G Ab A dim| Eb7  Bb7||
||E7  | A7  | E7  |E7  | A7  | A7  | E7  | E7  | B7  | A7  | E7 E/G# A A#| E7  B7 ||
||F7  | Bb7 | F7  |F7  | Bb7 | Bb7 | F7  | F7  | C7  | Bb7 | F7 F/A Bb7 Bdim.| F7  C7 ||
||F#7  | B7  | F#7 |F#7 | B7  | B7  | F#7 | F#7 | C#7 | B7  | F#7 F#/A B7 Cdim.| F#7  C#7 ||
||G7  | C7  | G7  |G7  | C7  | C7  | G7  | G7  | D7  | C7  | G7 G/B C7 C#dim.| G7  D7 ||
||Ab7  | Db7 |Ab7  |Ab7 |Db7  | Db7 | Ab7 | Ab7 | Eb7 |Db7  | Ab7 Ab/C Db7 Ddim.|Ab7 Eb7||
||A7  | D7  | A7  |A7  | D7  | D7  | A7  | A7  | E7  | D7  | A7 A/C# D7 D#dim.| A7  E7 ||
||Bb7  |Eb7  |Bb7  Bb7 | Eb7 | Eb7 | Bb7 | Bb7 | F7  | Eb7 | Bb7 Bb/D Eb7 Edim.|Bb7 F7 ||
||B7  | E7  | B7  |B7  | E7  | E7  | B7  | B7  | F#7 | E7  | B7 B/D# E7 Fdim.| B7  F#7 ||
```

The peculiar thing about a blues scale is that in a simple blues progression like the ones above the blues scale, which is built on the tonic (first tone) of the I chord, can be played over all of the chord changes and it will fit. You can hear many traditional blues recordings of artists like Muddy Waters, Howlin' Wolf, Chuck Berry, Little Walter, and many more playing this single scale over an entire progression. You can practice this progression with the Medium Shuffle with the CDs enclosed. The medium speed is the closest version to the old style blues shuffle.

Exercise: #7b: Fast blues progressions using substitution chords

We will now practice the final audio exercises with the fast blues progression and use the substitution chords throughout. The following exercises are blues progressions played one time in the starting key and then modulated down one whole step. This will take the reader through the blues in C,Bb,Ab,F#,E, and D. The progression is then repeated in Db,B,A,G,F, and Eb. You will have the opportunity to practice blues in all keys in a slow style, in a medium shuffle, and finally in a jazz bebop style.

BLUES WITH SUBSTITUTION CHORDS — Dave Rice

BLUES WITH SUBSTITUTION CHORDS P.2
55 G#m Gm7 C7 F#m7 Bm7 F9 E9 C#7 C13 B13
61 D7 G#13 G7 G#dim D7 Am7 G#13 G7 G#m7b5 C#7
67 F#m Fm7 B♭7 Em7 Am7 E♭9 D9 B7 B♭13 A13
73 D♭7 G13 G♭7 Gdim D♭7 A♭m7 G13 G♭7 Gm7b5 C7
79 Fm Em7 A7 E♭m7 A♭m7 D9 D♭9 B♭7 A13 A♭13
85 B7 F13 E7 Fdim B7 F#m7 F13 E7 Fm7b5 A#7
91 D#m Dm7 G7 C#m7 F#m7 C9 B9 G#7 G13 F#13
97 A7 D#13 D7 D#dim A7 Em7 D#13 D7 D#m7b5 G#7
103 C#m Cm7 F7 Bm7 Em7 B♭9 A9 F#7 F13 E13

Blues With Substitution Chords p.5
109 G7 C♯13 C7 C♯dim G7 Dm7 C♯13 C7 C♯m7b5 F♯7
115 Bm B♭m7 E♭7 Am7 Dm7 A♭9 G9 E7 E♭13 D13
121 F7 B13 B♭7 Bdim F7 Cm7 B13 B♭7 Bm7b5 E7
127 Am A♭m7 D♭7 Gm7 Cm7 G♭9 F9 D7 D♭13 C13
133 E♭7 A13 A♭7 Adim E♭7 B♭m7 A13 A♭7 Am7b5 D7
139 Gm G♭m7 B7 Fm7 B♭m7 E9 E♭9 C7 B13 B♭13

Blues With Substitution Chords B♭ — Dave Rice

Blues With Substitution Chords B, P.2

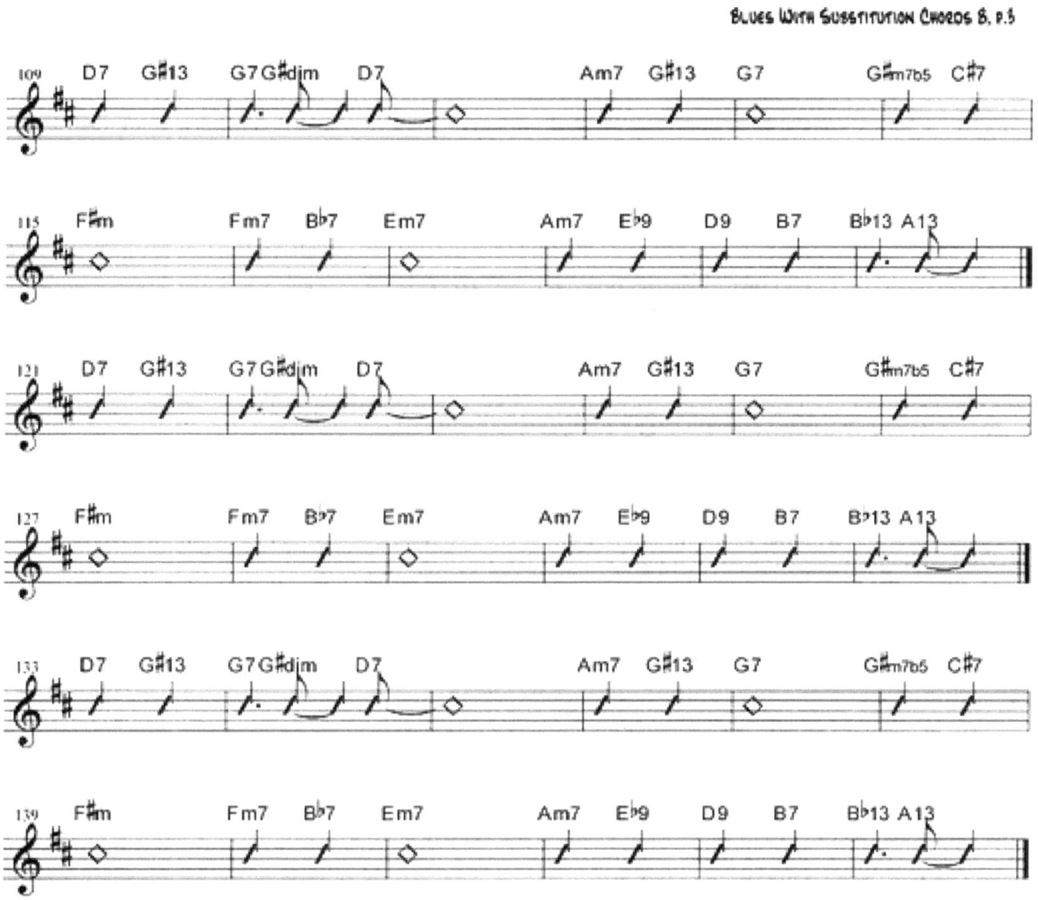
BLUES WITH SUBSTITUTION CHORDS B, P.3
109 D7 G#13 G7 G#dim D7 Am7 G#13 G7 G#m7b5 C#7
115 F#m Fm7 Bb7 Em7 Am7 Eb9 D9 B7 Bb13 A13
121 D7 G#13 G7 G#dim D7 Am7 G#13 G7 G#m7b5 C#7
127 F#m Fm7 Bb7 Em7 Am7 Eb9 D9 B7 Bb13 A13
133 D7 G#13 G7 G#dim D7 Am7 G#13 G7 G#m7b5 C#7
139 F#m Fm7 Bb7 Em7 Am7 Eb9 D9 B7 Bb13 A13

BLUES WITH SUBSTITUTION CHORDS E♭

Dave Rice

Blues With Substitution Chords E. p.2

Blues With Substitution Chords E, p.5
109 A7 D#13 D7 D#dim A7 Em7 D#13 D7 D#m7b5 G#7
115 C#m Cm7 F7 Bm7 Em7 Bb9 A9 F#7 F13 E13
121 A7 D#13 D7 D#dim A7 Em7 D#13 D7 D#m7b5 G#7
127 C#m Cm7 F7 Bm7 Em7 Bb9 A9 F#7 F13 E13
133 A7 D#13 D7 D#dim A7 Em7 D#13 D7 D#m7b5 G#7
139 C#m Cm7 F7 Bm7 Em7 Bb9 A9 F#7 F13 E13

BLUES WITH SUBSTITUTION CHORDS F

DAVE RICE

BLUES WITH SUBSTITUTION CHORDS F P.2
55 Bm Bbm7 Eb7 Am7 Dm7 Ab9 G9 E7 Eb13 D13
61 G7 C#13 C7 C#dim G7 Dm7 C#13 C7 C#m7b5 F#7
67 Bm Bbm7 Eb7 Am7 Dm7 Ab9 G9 E7 Eb13 D13
73 G7 C#13 C7 C#dim G7 Dm7 C#13 C7 C#m7b5 F#7
79 Bm Bbm7 Eb7 Am7 Dm7 Ab9 G9 E7 Eb13 D13
85 G7 C#13 C7 C#dim G7 Dm7 C#13 C7 C#m7b5 F#7
91 Bm Bbm7 Eb7 Am7 Dm7 Ab9 G9 E7 Eb13 D13
97 G7 C#13 C7 C#dim G7 Dm7 C#13 C7 C#m7b5 F#7
103 Bm Bbm7 Eb7 Am7 Dm7 Ab9 G9 E7 Eb13 D13

BLUES WITH SUBSTITUTION CHORDS F p.5

As you practice this progression remember that you have all of the resources from the ii-V7-I and ii⁻7-V7+-i library to choose from. You can utilize the modes, diminished scales, half diminished scales, altered scales, pentatonic scales in all the various positions.

Lesson 8: Jazz and Bepop

Now let's look at the blues which is used more in jazz and bebop. I once asked Herbie Hancock to show me a way to improve my jazz playing. He thought for a minute and replied, "I know a lot about substitution chords." The following progression begins with the same shift from the I chord to the IV and to the V7 but in between the main chord changes you will find passing chords such as iii7, VI7, ii7-V7 as well as substitution chords which are passing chords that sound the interval of a tri-tone away from the original chord. When you practice the slow and fast versions of the blues progression with the audio exercises which are included, each time you move to the next significant chord in the progression which is a perfect fourth away-ie-I7 IV7, or V7, first play a dominant 7th chord or 13th chord which has a root which is a raised 4th away and descend down to the destination chord. For example, when moving from C7 to an F7 , play the C7 and then play the F#7 or F#13th chord before moving to the F7. The F#13 is a substitution for the C7. This practice is used all the time in playing blues and taken to the extreme in bebop. The first time I learned about tri-tone substitution chords I was playing in St. Louis at a convention center where I met the keyboard player from the band The Fifth Dimension. He sat down and showed me the substitution chords for jazz blues and ii7-V7-I. He also showed me how to approach each chord with a ii7-V7 as a substitution. I remember immediately hearing all the great harmonies that I had heard in jazz recordings. We will examine a bebop blues progression in which we will use many substitution chords throughout the progression. As you practice this progression with the substitution chords, each time you play a seventh chord, play the minor chord which is a fourth away from the seventh chord. This makes the substitution chords and the progressions all ii7-V7 progressions. This opens up all the possibilities of soloing on top of the ii7-V7 and I in whatever function it may assume.

We can consider the iii-VI7 as a ii7-V7 of the ii and use the same modal, diminished, half diminished, altered scales and endless possibilities that are available to us. Play the following progressions along with the audio exercises the CD enclosed.

REFERENCES

Mode. (n.d.) Retrieved January 21,2008, from Wikipedia: http://en.wikipedia.org/wiki/Musical_mode
Improvise. (n.d.) Retrieved July 11, 2008, from http://www.sibeliuseducation.com/pdfs/MENC_tables.pdf
Standards. (n.d.) Retrieved June 21,2008 from
http://www.menc.org/publication/books/performance_standards/k-4.html
Kod·ly, Z & Kod·ly, Mrs.Z. (1974) "The Selected Writings of Zolt·n Kod·ly", Boosey & Hawkes Music Publishers Ltd. London WIA 1BR.
Landis, B.& Carder, P. (1972), "The Eclectic Curriculum in American Music Education: Contributions of Dalcroze, Kod·ly, and Orff", Music Educators National Conference 1201 Washington, D.C..

Levine, M. (1995). "The Jazz Theory Book", Sher Music Company., Petaluma, Ca.
Jarvis,J.& Beach, D.(2002). "The Jazz Educators Handbook". Kendor Music, Inc. Delevan, N.Y.
Aebersold, J.(1967). "How To Play Jazz and Improvise", Jamey Aebersold Jazz, Inc. New Albany ,In.
Baker,D.(1968) "Jazz Improvisation", Alfred Publishing Co, Inc. Van Nuys, Ca.
Aebersold, J.(1979)."Turnarounds, Cycles & II/V7's for all instruments" . Jamey Aebersold Jazz, New Albany ,In.
Haerle, D.(1974). "Jazz/Rock voicings for the contemporary Keyboard Player", (Haerle,Dan, 1974) forward by Jerry Coker. Haestudio P/R, Inc.Lebanon, In. 46052.
Haerle, D, Coker, J. (1974)."Jazz/rock contemporary voicings for the contemporary keyboard player". Studio P/R,Inc. Lebanon, In.
Haerle, D, Coker, J. (1974) ìJazz Improvisation for Keyboard Players Complete Editionî. Alfred Publishing Co. Inc. Van Nuys, Ca.

Additional References
Aebersold, J(1974) The II-V7-I progression, the most important musical sequence in jazz! Jamey Aebersold Jazz, New Albany ,In.
Aebersold, J(1974) The II-V7-I progression, the most important musical sequence in jazz![CD]. Jamey Aebersold Jazz, New Albany ,In.
Leibman,D Observations on the blues as cited in Aebersold, J(1981)Nothin' but the blues.
Wickipedia Online Dictionary, keywords 'chord' July 1,2007.
The New Grove Dictionary of Music and Musicians Fifth Edition (2001)Volume 5 Canon- Classic rock.
The New Grove Dictionary of Music and Musicians Fifth Edition (2001) Volume 7 D‡n tranh - Eg¸Ès, p. 442.
The New Grove Dictionary of Music and Musicians Fifth Edition (2001) Volume 7 D‡n tranh - Eg¸Ès, p. 351.
Singh, Vijay (2003). Where to Find Resources and Quality Teaching Tools, Repertoire & standards: vocal jazz-advocacy for jazz pedagogy p.47:Retrieved from IIMP database 6/28/2007.
The New Grove Dictionary of Music and Musicians Fifth Edition (2001). Volume 3 Baxter-Borosini, p. 727.
Leonard, H. (1980)."How to improvise with piano". Hal Leonard publishing, Inc. and Yamaha music foundation. Milwaukee, Wi.
LaPorta, J. (1972). A guide to jazz phrasing and interpretation. Berklee Press Publications.
High, J. (2005) Chords /scales and diagrammed approaches for improvisation. Authorhouse.
Blake,J, Jr.; Harmon, J.,Harmon,P. (1993), Jazz Improvisation Made Easy for Violin, Volume #1 Beginning to improvise. P.O.Box 186,301 Littleton Road, Westford, MA. 01886.
Azzara,C; Grunow, R; Edwin, G. (1997)Creativity in Improvisation. GIA publications, Inc.
Fitzgerald, M.; McCord, K.; Berg, S. (2003) Chop-Monster Jr.,jazz language tutor for general music instruction. Alfred Publishing Co. Inc. 16320 Roscoe Blvd., Suite 100 P.O. Box 10003 Van Nuys, Ca. 91410-0003.